IT'

MW01701421

The Unclaimed Property Resource Guide©

Knowledge In Motion® and **IT'$ YOUR MONEY®** are registered trademarks of Knowledge In Motion®, Inc.

Knowledge In Motion®, Inc.
1825 Ponce de Leon Blvd., Suite 239
Coral Gables, Florida 33134-4418
USA

Tel: (305) 441-0610
Fax: (305) 446-4911
E-mail: info@unclaimed-property.com

Contents

APPENDIX

This resource guide

is dedicated to the

PUBLIC EDUCATION

and

AWARENESS

of

UNCLAIMED PROPERTY.

Section I:

Introduction to Unclaimed Property

(This page intentionally blank)

How Money and Property Becomes Unclaimed

Did you ever…

- open a school savings account as a child or for your own child and then forget about it?
- move without getting your utility deposit refund?
- forget to cash a health insurance check?
- neglect to cash interest or dividend checks on a security?
- leave a job and never go back to get your last pay check?
- fail to notify companies who owe you money that you have moved?

In cases like these and many others, your money is eventually turned over to the State.

State laws require banks, insurance companies, utilities and other businesses to turn dormant savings accounts, unclaimed insurance and stock dividends, and other inactive holdings over to the State. If there has been no activity in the account for a set period of time, usually between two and five years, your money is considered unclaimed or abandoned.

Before unclaimed funds are turned over to the State, banks and insurance companies attempt to notify you. Despite these efforts, many funds remain unclaimed and are turned over to the State Comptroller or Treasurer.

The State holds unclaimed funds in trust - with the State Comptroller or Treasurer as custodian - until the funds are claimed by the owner or heir. The State never takes ownership of the money. It is held for you until you claim it. If at any time you can prove this money is yours, the State will return it to you without charge.

The History of Unclaimed Property

"The origin of the unclaimed property law dates back as far as the colonization of America. Since that time, states have revised and refined their various unclaimed property laws, resulting in over $10 billion in collections for the benefit of owners whose whereabouts are at least temporarily unknown.

The custodial nature of the unclaimed property law obliges each state to maintain unclaimed funds and related owner information for claim by the rightful owner.

All states make a diligent effort to locate and refund these funds to the rightful owner, at no cost to the owner."[1]

[1] National Association of Unclaimed Property Administrators

(This page intentionally blank)

What is Unclaimed Property?

Currently, over **$35 billion** in unclaimed property is held by state and federal agencies across the United States. **One in eight Americans is owed unclaimed property**.

Unclaimed property may include:

- ☑ Savings and checking accounts
- ☑ Uncashed payroll checks
- ☑ Cashiers checks
- ☑ Money orders
- ☑ Travelers checks
- ☑ Certificates of deposit
- ☑ Customer deposits
- ☑ Customer overpayments
- ☑ Paid up life insurance policies
- ☑ Health insurance payments
- ☑ Accident insurance payments
- ☑ Uncashed death benefit checks
- ☑ Gift certificates

- ☑ Christmas club accounts
- ☑ Stock and dividends
- ☑ Utility deposits
- ☑ Oil and gas royalty payments
- ☑ Safe deposit box contents

…and many other dormant financial assets.

Where is Unclaimed Property Held?

An important U.S. Supreme Court decision, Texas vs. New Jersey, 379 U.S. 674 (1965), provides a guideline in deciding where unclaimed property is held. Briefly summarizing;

> **...unclaimed property is to be returned to the state of the property owner's last known address. If there is no owner's address associated with the property, then it should be returned to the state in which the business remitting the funds is incorporated.**

Thus, states regularly exchange property and related information; this is known as **reciprocity**.

(This page intentionally blank)

Locating Owners of Unclaimed Property

One of the central functions of each state's unclaimed property division is reuniting owners with unclaimed property.

Along with the legal requirements within each state, states continue to enhance owner location efforts through statewide outreach activities such as public appearances at shopping malls or fairs, public service announcements and unclaimed property programs on radio and television.

In order to obtain current address matches, many states initiate computer matches with their respective Department of Revenue or Department of Motor Vehicles. Additionally, some states are able to receive current address information through contacts with various credit bureaus. These efforts result in a greater public awareness of the unclaimed property programs and result in an increasing percentage of unclaimed property being returned to the rightful owner or heir.

Claimants are encouraged to contact and work with each state, as claims processing is a public service to the owner. The continued emphasis on the interstate cooperation helps the claimant avoid time consuming and often confusing referrals.

Who May Claim This Property?

All states have specific procedures and forms to use when claiming unclaimed property; and nearly all states maintain the unclaimed property as custodian forever.

The turnaround time for an unclaimed property claim may vary, however, states attempt to expedite claims in a timely manner when sufficient ownership documentation is provided.

Often a claim requires a review and approval by more than one agency, or payment is issued by an agency which is not associated with the program administration. States offer assistance to eliminate unnecessary delays in documentation requests and payment. Some of the most common reasons for delays in processing are:

- Claim form is not signed by claimant, or signature is not notarized;
- No identification is presented by claimant;
- No supporting proof of ownership is filed with the claim;

- There is insufficient information available to verify property ownership;

- Some states issue an annual listing of owners of unclaimed property in regional newspapers which causes an influx of claim-related inquiries and processing requirements;

- Additionally, states have reporting deadlines for businesses to follow when remitting unclaimed property to them. These peak periods of reporting and owner notification can have an impact on the time frame needed to process a claim for approval.

Am I owed Unclaimed Property?

One in eight Americans is owed unclaimed property. Most people are unaware that they are owed or may be entitled to unclaimed property. Something as simple as an incorrect or change of address, a misspelled or change of name - for these reasons and many more, the rightful owner cannot be located and the property would be deemed unclaimed and subsequently transferred to the appropriate agency for safe keeping.

Agencies holding unclaimed property do attempt to locate the rightful owners. However, in most cases and for the above reasons, efforts to find the rightful owner are unsuccessful.

Remember, it's easy for you to find them, it may be impossible for them to find you. Therefore, you should contact state and federal agencies yourself and request they search their files for unclaimed property in your name. And remember, state and federal agencies receive **hundreds of millions of dollars** in additional unclaimed **property each and every year**, so you should inquire every year or two.

(This page intentionally blank)

Section II:

Unclaimed Property Resources

(This page intentionally blank)

Internet Resources

Over the last year or two the Internet has become an essential tool for research by both businesses and individuals alike. The Internet provides ease of access to literally hundreds of millions of documents and resources from around the world.

IT'$ YOUR MONEY®, The National Unclaimed Property Database© Internet site was launched in July, 1996. Our Internet site provides the public with a **FREE centralized**, search database of unclaimed property from across the United States. The centralization of this vast number of local, national and international sources of unclaimed money and property provides a single research location for individuals and businesses alike.

The National Unclaimed Property Database© is continually updated. In addition, new sources of local, national and international unclaimed property are being identified for future inclusion.

Visit our Internet site today.

http://www.unclaimed-property.com

(This page intentionally blank)

United States - State Agencies

All states have enacted statutes which govern property deemed unclaimed. While statutes vary from state to state, each state has established an Unclaimed Property Office or Division. These offices will be the starting point on your search for unclaimed property.

Depending upon the agency, you may call, write or fax a request that they search their records for your name. We recommend you write to the agencies so you may include all pertinent information including previous addresses, maiden name, and business name if applicable. The more information you provide, the more thorough the agencies' search.

In most cases, you will begin receiving written responses from the agencies within two to three weeks. If unclaimed property is found in your name, the state will send you a claim form and specific instructions on how to claim your property.

Keep in mind the following two important points:

1. States practice "**reciprocity**", whereby unclaimed property is returned to the

state of the property owner's **last known address**. If there is no owner's address associated with the property, then the property is **returned to the state** in which the originating business remitting the property is incorporated. **Therefore, even if you have not resided in nor did business in a certain state, that does not preclude them from holding property in your name**.

For example: John Doe lived in the state of Georgia his entire life and was employed by the Atlanta Division of the XYZ Company whose corporate headquarters were in Chicago, Illinois. John Doe moved out of Atlanta and forgot to pick up his last pay check. The XYZ Company did not have his new address and could not deliver this pay check to him, since the "last known address" for John Doe was incorrect. Thus the funds became "unclaimed". Even though John Doe resided in the state of Georgia his entire life, the funds were turned over to the unclaimed property agency of the state of the corporate headquarters of XYZ Company - the **State of Illinois**.

2. Hundreds of millions of dollars in additional unclaimed property are reported to state **agencies each and every year**. Check state agencies every year or two to see if your name appears on their updated unclaimed property file.

The following pages provide contact information for all state agencies of the United States (including the District of Columbia and Puerto Rico) inclusive of mailing and Internct address, telephone and facsimile numbers, and current quantities and dollar values for unclaimed property held by each agency.

Later in this guide you will find a sample letter which you may wish to use as a template for your written inquiries to these agencies.

State of Alabama

State of Alabama
Unclaimed Property Division
PO Box 302520
Montgomery, AL 36130-2520

Telephone: 334-242-9614
Facsimile: 334-242-9620

Internet address
WWW: http://www.unclaimed-property.com

Agency: Pending
E-mail: Pending

Unclaimed Property records
Quantity: 140,000
Value: $54,000,000

State of Alaska

State of Alaska, Department of Revenue
Unclaimed Property Section
PO Box 110420
Juneau, AK 99811-0420

Telephone: 907-465-4653
Facsimile: 907-465-2375

Internet address
WWW: http://www.unclaimed-property.com

Agency: http://www.revenue.state.ak.us
E-mail: unclaimed_property@revenue.state.ak.us

Unclaimed Property records
Quantity: 25,000
Value: $9,000,000

State of Arizona

State of Arizona, Department of Revenue
Unclaimed Property Unit
1600 West Monroe
Phoenix, AZ 85007-2650

Telephone: 602-542-4643
Facsimile: 602-542-4667

Internet address
WWW: http://www.unclaimed-property.com

Agency: Pending
E-mail: Pending

Unclaimed Property records
Quantity: 300,000
Value: $72,000,000

State of Arkansas

State of Arkansas, Auditor of State
Unclaimed Property Division
1400 West 3rd, Suite 100
Little Rock, AR 72201-1811

Telephone: 501-682-9174
800-252-4648
Facsimile: 501-682-6005

Internet address
WWW: http://www.unclaimed-property.com

Agency: Pending
E-mail: Pending

Unclaimed Property records
Quantity: 35,000
Value: $14,000,000

State of California

State of California, Division of Collections
Bureau of Unclaimed Property
PO Box 942850
Sacramento, CA 94250-5873

Telephone:	916-445-8318
	916-323-2857
Facsimile:	916-322-9163

Internet address

WWW:	http://www.unclaimed-property.com
Agency:	http://www.sco.ca.gov
E-mail:	Pending

Unclaimed Property records

Quantity:	4,600,000
Value:	$1,900,000,000

State of Colorado

State of Colorado
Unclaimed Property Division
1560 Broadway, Suite 1225
Denver, CO 80202

Telephone: 303-894-2443
Facsimile: 303-894-2351

Internet address
WWW: http://www.unclaimed-property.com

Agency: http://www.treasurer.state.co.us
E-mail: Pending

Unclaimed Property records
Quantity: 20,000
Value: $75,000,000

State of Connecticut

State of Connecticut
Unclaimed Property Unit
55 Elm Street
Hartford, CT 06106

Telephone:	860-702-3050
	800-833-7318
Facsimile:	860-702-3044

Internet address

WWW:	http://www.unclaimed-property.com
Agency:	http://www.state.ct.us
E-mail:	unclaimed.property@po.state.ct.us

Unclaimed Property records

Quantity:	1,200,000
Value:	$250,000,000

State of Delaware

State of Delaware
Delaware State Escheater
PO Box 8931
Wilmington, DE 19899-8931

Telephone: 302-577-3349
Facsimile: 302-577-3689

Internet address
WWW: http://www.unclaimed-property.com

Agency: Pending
E-mail: Pending

Unclaimed Property records
Quantity: 1,250,000
Value: $500,000,000

District of Columbia

District of Columbia, Office of the Comptroller
Unclaimed Property Unit
415 12th Street NW, Room 408
Washington, DC 20004

Telephone: 202-727-0063
Facsimile: 202-727-2389

Internet address
WWW: http://www.unclaimed-property.com

Agency: Pending
E-mail: Pending

Unclaimed Property records
Quantity: 100,000
Value: $40,000,000

State of Florida

State of Florida, Department of Banking and Finance
Abandoned Property Division
101 East Gaines Street
Tallahassee, FL 32399-0350

Telephone: 904-488-0357
888-258-2253
Facsimile: 904-488-9728

Internet address
WWW: http://www.unclaimed-property.com

Agency: http://www.dbf.state.fl.us
E-mail: Pending

Unclaimed Property records
Quantity: 3,000,000
Value: $450,000,000

State of Georgia

State of Georgia
Property Tax Division, Unclaimed Property
270 Washington Street, Room 404
Atlanta, GA 30334-9009

Telephone: 404-656-4244
Facsimile: 404-651-8689

Internet address
WWW: http://www.unclaimed-property.com

Agency: Pending
E-mail: Pending

Unclaimed Property records
Quantity: 750,000
Value: $190,000,000

State of Hawaii

State of Hawaii
Unclaimed Property Section
PO Box 150
Honolulu, HI 96810-0150

Telephone: 808-586-1589
Facsimile: 808-586-1644

Internet address
WWW: http://www.unclaimed-property.com

Agency: Pending
E-mail: Pending

Unclaimed Property records
Quantity: 200,000
Value: $40,000,000

State of Idaho

State of Idaho, State Tax Commission
Unclaimed Property Section
PO Box 36, 800 Park Plaza IV
Boise, ID 83722-2240

Telephone: 208-334-7623
Facsimile: 208-334-7655

Internet address
WWW: http://www.unclaimed-property.com

Agency: Pending
E-mail: Pending

Unclaimed Property records
Quantity: 84,000
Value: $18,000,000

State of Illinois

State of Illinois, Unclaimed Property Division
Department of Financial Institutions
PO Box 19495
Springfield, IL 62794-9495

Telephone: 217-785-6995
Facsimile: 217-785-6999

Internet address
WWW: http://www.unclaimed-property.com

Agency: http://www.state.il.us
E-mail: Pending

Unclaimed Property records
Quantity: 3,400,000
Value: $600,000,000

State of Indiana

State of Indiana, Attorney Generals Office
Unclaimed Property Division
402 West Washington, Suite C-531
Indianapolis, IN 46204-2770

Telephone: 317-232-6348
Facsimile: 317-232-7979

Internet address
WWW: http://www.unclaimed-property.com

Agency: http://www.state.in.us
E-mail: E-mail form available on web site

Unclaimed Property records
Quantity: 200,000
Value: $40,000,000

State of Iowa

State of Iowa, Treasurer
Unclaimed Property Division
State Capitol Building
Des Moines, IA 50319-0005

Telephone: 515-281-5367
Facsimile: 515-281-6962

Internet address
WWW: http://www.unclaimed-property.com

Agency: Pending
E-mail: Pending

Unclaimed Property records
Quantity: 300,000
Value: $20,000,000

State of Kansas

State of Kansas
Unclaimed Property Division
900 SW Jackson, Suite 201
Topeka, KS 66612-1235

Telephone: 785-296-4165
Facsimile: 785-291-3172

Internet address
WWW: http://www.unclaimed-property.com

Agency: http://www.treasurer.state.ks.us
E-mail: unclaimed@www.treasurer.state.ks.us

Unclaimed Property records
Quantity: 340,000
Value: $68,000,000

State of Kentucky

State of Kentucky, Unclaimed Property Branch
Kentucky State Treasury Department
Suite 183, Capitol Annex
Frankfort, KY 40601

Telephone: 502-564-4722
Facsimile: 502-564-6545

Internet address
WWW: http://www.unclaimed-property.com

Agency: Pending
E-mail: Pending

Unclaimed Property records
Quantity: 90,000
Value: $40,000,000

State of Louisiana

State of Louisiana, Unclaimed Property Section
Louisiana Department of Revenue and Taxation
PO Box 91010
Baton Rouge, LA 70821-9010

Telephone: 504-925-7407
Facsimile: 504-925-3896

Internet address
WWW: http://www.unclaimed-property.com

Agency: http://www.rev.state.la.us
E-mail: Pending

Unclaimed Property records
Quantity: 275,000
Value: $110,000,000

State of Maine

State of Maine, Treasury Department
Abandoned Property Division
39 State House Station
Augusta, ME 04333-0039

Telephone: 207-287-6668
Facsimile: 207-287-2367

Internet address
WWW: http://www.unclaimed-property.com

Agency: Pending
E-mail: Pending

Unclaimed Property records
Quantity: 70,000
Value: $25,000,000

State of Maryland

State of Maryland
Unclaimed Property Section
301 West Preston Street
Baltimore, MD 21201-2385

Telephone:	410-767-1700
	800-782-7383
Facsimile:	410-333-7150

Internet address

WWW:	http://www.unclaimed-property.com
Agency:	http://www.comp.state.md.us
E-mail:	unclaimed@comp.state.md.us

Unclaimed Property records

Quantity:	260,000
Value:	$68,000,000

State of Massachusetts

State of Massachusetts
Abandoned Property Division
1 Ashburton Place, 12th Floor
Boston, MA 02108

Telephone: 617-367-0400
Facsimile: 617-248-3944

Internet address
WWW: http://www.unclaimed-property.com

Agency: http://www.magnet.state.ma.us
E-mail: Pending

Unclaimed Property records
Quantity: 8,000,000
Value: $715,000,000

State of Michigan

State of Michigan, Department of Treasury
Abandoned and Unclaimed Property Division
Lansing, MI 48922

Telephone: 517-335-4327
Facsimile: 517-335-4400

Internet address
WWW: http://www.unclaimed-property.com

Agency: Pending
E-mail: Pending

Unclaimed Property records
Quantity: 3,000,000
Value: $322,000,000

State of Minnesota

State of Minnesota, Unclaimed Property Section
Minnesota Commerce Department
133 East 7th Street
St. Paul, MN 55101

Telephone:	612-296-2568
	800-925-5668
Facsimile:	612-296-8591

Internet address

WWW:	http://www.unclaimed-property.com

Agency:	Pending
E-mail:	Pending

Unclaimed Property records

Quantity:	200,000
Value:	$75,000,000

State of Mississippi

State of Mississippi
Unclaimed Property Division
PO Box 138
Jackson, MS 39205-0138

Telephone: 601-359-3600
Facsimile: 601-359-2001

Internet address
WWW: http://www.unclaimed-property.com

Agency: http://www.treasury.state.ms.us
E-mail: Pending

Unclaimed Property records
Quantity: 29,000
Value: $10,000,000

State of Missouri

State of Missouri
Unclaimed Property Division
PO Box 1272
Jefferson City, MO 65102-1272

Telephone: 573-751-0840
Facsimile: 573-526-6027

Internet address
WWW: http://www.unclaimed-property.com

Agency: http://www.sto.state.mo.us
E-mail: upropert@mail.state.mo.us

Unclaimed Property records
Quantity: 550,000
Value: $112,000,000

State of Montana

State of Montana, Department of Revenue
Unclaimed Property Section
PO Box 5805, Mitchell Building
Helena, MT 59604-5805

Telephone: 406-444-2425
Facsimile: 406-444-0750

Internet address
WWW: http://www.unclaimed-property.com

Agency: Pending
E-mail: Pending

Unclaimed Property records
Quantity: 200,000
Value: $17,000,000

State of Nebraska

State of Nebraska
Unclaimed Property Division
PO Box 94788, Capitol Building
Lincoln, NE 68509-4788

Telephone: 402-471-2455
Facsimile: 402-471-4390

Internet address
WWW: http://www.unclaimed-property.com

Agency: Pending
E-mail: Pending

Unclaimed Property records
Quantity: 60,000
Value: $25,000,000

State of Nevada

State of Nevada
Unclaimed Property Division
2501 East Sahara Avenue, Suite 304
Las Vegas, NV 89104-4104

Telephone: 702-486-4140
Facsimile: 702-486-4177

Internet address
WWW: http://www.unclaimed-property.com

Agency: http://www.state.nv.us
E-mail: updnevst@govmail.state.nv.us

Unclaimed Property records
Quantity: 140,000
Value: $40,000,000

State of New Hampshire

State of New Hampshire, Treasury Department
Abandoned Property Division
25 Capitol Street, Room 205
Concord, NH 03301

Telephone: 603-271-2649
Facsimile: 603-271-2730

Internet address
WWW: http://www.unclaimed-property.com

Agency: http://www.state.nh.us
E-mail: Pending

Unclaimed Property records
Quantity: 50,000
Value: $20,000,000

State of New Jersey

State of New Jersey, Department of the Treasury
Property Administration
CN 214
Trenton, NJ 08646-0214

Telephone:	609-984-8234
	609-292-1652
Facsimile:	609-292-9439

Internet address

WWW:	http://www.unclaimed-property.com
Agency:	Pending
E-mail:	Pending

Unclaimed Property records

Quantity:	1,250,000
Value:	$500,000,000

State of New Mexico

State of New Mexico
Taxation and Revenue Department
PO Box 25123
Santa Fe, NM 87504-5123

Telephone:	505-827-0767
	505-827-0769
Facsimile:	505-827-1759

Internet address

WWW:	http://www.unclaimed-property.com

Agency:	Pending
E-mail:	Pending

Unclaimed Property records

Quantity:	163,000
Value:	$45,000,000

State of New York

State of New York
Office of Unclaimed Funds
Alfred E. Smith Building, 9th Floor
Albany, NY 12236

Telephone:	518-474-4038
Facsimile:	518-473-2177

Internet address

WWW:	http://www.unclaimed-property.com
Agency:	http://www.osc.state.ny.us
E-mail:	nys-unclaimed-funds@osc.state.ny.us

Unclaimed Property records

Quantity:	11,000,000
Value:	$3,600,000,000

State of North Carolina

State of North Carolina
Escheat and Unclaimed Property
325 North Salisbury Street
Raleigh, NC 27603-1385

Telephone: 919-733-6876
Facsimile: 919-715-0229

Internet address
WWW: http://www.unclaimed-property.com

Agency: http://www.treasurer.state.nc.us
E-mail: Pending

Unclaimed Property records
Quantity: 625,000
Value: $160,000,000

State of North Dakota

State of North Dakota, State Land Department
Unclaimed Property Division
PO Box 5523, 1707 North 9th Street
Bismarck, ND 58506-5523

Telephone: 701-328-2805
Facsimile: 701-328-3650

Internet address
WWW: http://www.unclaimed-property.com

Agency: http://www.land.state.nd.us
E-mail: Pending

Unclaimed Property records
Quantity: 14,000
Value: $10,000,000

State of Ohio

State of Ohio
Division of Unclaimed Funds
77 South High Street, 20th Floor
Columbus, OH 43266-0545

Telephone: 614-466-4433
Facsimile: 614-752-5078

Internet address
WWW: http://www.unclaimed-property.com

Agency: http://www.state.oh.us
E-mail: Pending

Unclaimed Property records
Quantity: 1,600,000
Value: $150,000,000

State of Oklahoma

State of Oklahoma, Oklahoma Tax Commission
Unclaimed Property Section
2501 Lincoln Boulevard
Oklahoma City, OK 73194-0010

Telephone: 405-521-4275
405-521-4280
Facsimile: 405-521-2146

Internet address
WWW: http://www.unclaimed-property.com

Agency: Pending
E-mail: unclaimprop@mailhost.oktax.state.ok.us

Unclaimed Property records
Quantity: 600,000
Value: $80,000,000

State of Oregon

State of Oregon
Unclaimed Property Unit
775 Summer Street, N.E.
Salem, OR 97310

Telephone: 503-378-3805
Facsimile: 503-378-4844

Internet address
WWW: http://www.unclaimed-property.com

Agency: Pending
E-mail: Pending

Unclaimed Property records
Quantity: 150,000
Value: $56,000,000

State of Pennsylvania

State of Pennsylvania, State Treasurer
Office of Unclaimed Property
PO Box 1837
Harrisburg, PA 17105-1837

Telephone: 800-222-2046
Facsimile: 717-787-9079

Internet address
WWW: http://www.unclaimed-property.com

Agency: http://www.libertynet.org/~patreas/
E-mail: Pending

Unclaimed Property records
Quantity: 750,000
Value: $300,000,000

Puerto Rico

Puerto Rico
Treasury Department
PO Box 9024140
San Juan, PR 00902-4140

Telephone: 787-721-2020
Facsimile: Not released

Internet address
WWW: http://www.unclaimed-property.com

Agency: Pending
E-mail: Pending

Unclaimed Property records
Quantity: Not released
Value: Not released

State of Rhode Island

State of Rhode Island
Unclaimed Property Division
PO Box 1435
Providence, RI 02901-1435

Telephone: 401-277-6505
Facsimile: 401-274-3865

Internet address
WWW: http://www.unclaimed-property.com

Agency: http://www.state.ri.us
E-mail: ups@treasury.state.ri.us

Unclaimed Property records
Quantity: 60,000
Value: $60,000,000

State of South Carolina

State of South Carolina, State Treasurers Office
Unclaimed Property Division
PO Box 11778
Columbia, SC 29211-1778

Telephone: 803-737-4771
Facsimile: 803-343-0177

Internet address
WWW: http://www.unclaimed-property.com

Agency: Pending
E-mail: Pending

Unclaimed Property records
Quantity: 500,000
Value: $54,000,000

State of South Dakota

State of South Dakota
Unclaimed Property Division
500 East Capitol Avenue
Pierre, SD 57501-5070

Telephone: 605-773-3378
Facsimile: 605-773-3115

Internet address
WWW: http://www.unclaimed-property.com

Agency: Pending
E-mail: unclprop@st-treas.state.sd.us

Unclaimed Property records
Quantity: 20,000
Value: $8,000,000

State of Tennessee

State of Tennessee
Unclaimed Property Division
Andrew Jackson Building, 9th Floor
Nashville, TN 37243-0242

Telephone:	615-741-6499
Facsimile:	615-532-4979

Internet address

WWW:	http://www.unclaimed-property.com
Agency:	http://www.state.tn.us
E-mail:	unclaimed.property@mail.state.tn.us

Unclaimed Property records

Quantity:	200,000
Value:	$80,000,000

State of Texas

State of Texas, Comptroller of Public Accounts
Unclaimed Property Section
PO Box 12019
Austin, TX 78711-2019

Telephone:	512-463-3120
	512-475-1610
Facsimile:	512-936-6224

Internet address

WWW:	http://www.unclaimed-property.com
Agency:	http://www.window.state.tx.us
E-mail:	unclaimed.property@cpa.state.tx.us

Unclaimed Property records

Quantity:	3,300,000
Value:	$900,000,000

State of Utah

State of Utah, State Treasurers Office
Unclaimed Property Division
341 South Main Street, 5th Floor
Salt Lake City, UT 84111

Telephone: 801-320-5360
Facsimile: 801-533-4096

Internet address
WWW: http://www.unclaimed-property.com

Agency: http://www.treasurer.state.ut.us
E-mail: stupmain.ucprop@state.ut.us

Unclaimed Property records
Quantity: 75,000
Value: $30,000,000

State of Vermont

State of Vermont
Abandoned Property Division
133 State Street
Montepelier, VT 05633-6200

Telephone:	802-828-2407
	800-642-3191
Facsimile:	802-828-2772

Internet address

WWW:	http://www.unclaimed-property.com
Agency:	http://www.cit.state.vt.us
E-mail:	Pending

Unclaimed Property records

Quantity:	35,000
Value:	$5,000,000

State of Virginia

State of Virginia, Department of Treasury
Division of Unclaimed Property
PO Box 2478
Richmond, VA 23218-2478

Telephone: 804-225-2393
800-468-1088
Facsimile: 804-786-4653

Internet address
WWW: http://www.unclaimed-property.com

Agency: Pending
E-mail: Pending

Unclaimed Property records
Quantity: 750,000
Value: $300,000,000

State of Washington

State of Washington
Unclaimed Property Section
PO Box 448
Olympia, WA 98507-0448

Telephone: 360-586-2736
Facsimile: 360-586-2163

Internet address
WWW: http://www.unclaimed-property.com

Agency: http://www.wa.gov
E-mail: Pending

Unclaimed Property records
Quantity: Not released
Value: $220,000,000

State of West Virginia

State of West Virginia, Office of State Treasurer
Unclaimed Property Division
Capitol Complex
Charleston, WV 25305

Telephone: 304-343-4000
Facsimile: 304-558-4835

Internet address
WWW: http://www.unclaimed-property.com

Agency: Pending
E-mail: Pending

Unclaimed Property records
Quantity: 115,000
Value: $15,000,000

State of Wisconsin

State of Wisconsin, State Treasurers Office
Unclaimed Property Division
PO Box 2114
Madison, WI 53701-2114

Telephone: 608-267-7977
Facsimile: 608-261-6799

Internet address
WWW: http://www.unclaimed-property.com

Agency: http://badger.state.wi.us
E-mail: unclaim@mail.state.wi.us

Unclaimed Property records
Quantity: 200,000
Value: $75,000,000

State of Wyoming

State of Wyoming, State Treasurers Office
Unclaimed Property Division
1st Floor West, Herschler Building
22 W. 25th Street
Cheyenne, WY 82002

Telephone: 307-777-5590
Facsimile: 307-777-5430

Internet address
WWW: http://www.unclaimed-property.com

Agency: http://www.state.wy.us
E-mail: Pending

Unclaimed Property records
Quantity: 35,000
Value: $5,400,000

(This page intentionally blank)

United States - State Income Taxes

All states except Alaska, Florida, Nevada, South Dakota, Texas, Washington and Wyoming collect personal income taxes.

Unclaimed refund checks which were undeliverable are returned by the U.S. Postal Service to the originating states treasury or revenue department.

Alabama
Department of Revenue, Income Tax Division
PO Box 327410
Montgomery, AL 36132-7410
Tel: 334-242-1000 **Fax**: 334-242-0550

Alaska
No state income tax.

Arizona
Arizona Department of Revenue
PO Box 29086
Phoenix, AZ 85038-9086
Tel: 602-255-3381 **Fax**: 602-542-4765

Arkansas
Department of Finance and Administration
PO Box 1272
Little Rock, AR 72203
Tel: 501-682-7751 **Fax**: 501-682-1691

California
State of California
Franchise Tax Board
PO Box 942867
Sacramento, CA 94267-0041
Tel: 800-852-5711 **Fax**: 916-369-5340

Colorado
Taxpayer Services Division
Colorado Department of Revenue
1375 Sherman Street, #186
Denver, CO 80261
Tel: 303-232-2416 **Fax**: 303-866-3211

Connecticut
Department of Revenue Services
Taxpayer Services Division
25 Sigourney Street
Hartford, CT 06106
Tel: 203-297-5962 **Fax**: 203-297-5714

Delaware
Delaware Division of Revenue
Carvel State Office Building
820 N. French Street
Wilmington, DE 19801
Tel: 302-577-3300 **Fax**: 302-577-3689

District of Columbia
Department of Finance and Revenue
Taxpayer Assistance Division
441 4th Street N.W., #550N
Washington, DC 20001
Tel: 202-727-6104 **Fax**: 202-727-9069

Florida
No state income tax.

Georgia
State of Georgia
Department of Revenue
270 Washington Street S.W., #213
Atlanta, GA 30334
Tel: 404-656-4188 **Fax**: 404-651-9490

Hawaii
Department of Taxation
Taxpayer Service
830 Punchbowl Street, Middle Court
PO Box 259
Honolulu, HI 96809
Tel: 808-587-4242 **Fax**: Not Released

Idaho
State Tax Commission
800 Park Boulevard, Plaza IV
Boise, ID 83722
Tel: 208-334-7660 **Fax**: 208-334-7844

Illinois
Department of Revenue
101 W. Jefferson Street
Springfield, IL 62794
Tel: 217-785-2602 **Fax**: 217-782-6337

Indiana
Department of Revenue
Tax Policy Division
100 N. Senate, #N105
Indianapolis, IN 46204-2253
Tel: 317-232-2240 **Fax**: Not Released

Iowa
Department of Revenue and Finance
Taxpayer Services Division and Information
Hoover State Office Building
Des Moines, IA 50319
Tel: 515-281-3114 **Fax**: 515-242-6040

Kansas
Department of Revenue
Division of Taxation, Tax Assistant
Docking State Office Building
915 SW Harrison Street
Topeka, KS 66625-0001
Tel: 913-296-0222 **Fax**: 913-291-3614

Kentucky
Commonwealth of Kentucky
Revenue Cabinet, Taxpayer Ombudsman
PO Box 930, Station #15
Frankfort, KY 40602-0930
Tel: 502-564-7822 **Fax**: 502-564-8296

Louisiana
State of Louisiana
Department of Revenue and Taxation
PO Box 201
Baton Rouge, LA 70821-7537
Tel: 504-925-7537 **Fax**: 504-925-7641

Maine
State of Maine
Income tax Division, Bureau of Taxation
State House Station #24
Augusta, ME 04333
Tel: 207-626-8475 **Fax**: 207-287-4028

Maryland
State of Maryland
Comptroller of the Treasury, Income Tax Division
State Income Tax Building
Annapolis, MD 21411
Tel: 410-974-3981 **Fax**: 410-974-5808

Massachusetts
Commonwealth of Massachusetts
Department of Revenue
Leverette Saltonstall Building
100 Cambridge Street
Boston, MA 02204
Tel: 617-727-4545 **Fax**: 617-626-4150

Michigan
Income Tax Division
Michigan Department of Treasury
Treasury Building
Lansing, MI 48922
Tel: 517-373-3196 **Fax**: 517-373-4023

Minnesota
Department of Revenue
Taxpayer Assistance
Mail Station 4453
St. Paul, MN 55146
Tel: 612-296-3781 **Fax**: 612-297-7430

Mississippi
State Tax Commission
102 Woolfolk Building
PO Box 1033
Jackson, MS 39215
Tel: 601-359-1105 **Fax**: 601-359-6516

Missouri
Missouri Department of Revenue
Division of Taxation and Collection
PO Box 629
Jefferson City, MO 65505-0629
Tel: 573-751-3505 **Fax**: 573-751-7273

Montana
Department of Revenue
Income and Miscellaneous Tax Assistance
Capitol Station, Box 5805
Helena, MT 59620
Tel: 406-444-3674 **Fax**: 406-444-6642

Nebraska
Department of Revenue
Taxpayer Assistance
PO Box 94818
Lincoln, NE 68509
Tel: 402-471-2971 **Fax**: 402-471-5608

Nevada
No state income tax.

New Hampshire
Department of Revenue Administration
PO Box 457
Concord, NH 03302
Tel: 603-271-2318 **Fax**: 603-271-6121

New Jersey
State of New Jersey
Department of Revenue
Document Control Center
Trenton, NJ 08646
Tel: 609-588-2200 **Fax**: Not Released

New Mexico
Taxation and Revenue Department
PO Box 630
Santa Fe, NM 87509-0630
Tel: 505-827-0700 **Fax**: 505-827-0940

New York
Department of Taxation and Finance
Central Photocopy Unit
W.A. Harriman Campus
Albany, NY 12227
Tel: 518-457-7177 **Fax**: 518-457-7427

North Carolina
North Carolina Department of Revenue
Office Services Division
PO Box 25000
Raleigh, NC 27640
Tel: 919-733-4684 **Fax**: Not Released

North Dakota
Office of the State Tax Commissioner
State Capitol
600 E. Boulevard Avenue
Bismarck, ND 58505-0599
Tel: 701-328-2770 **Fax**: 701-328-3700

Ohio
Department of Taxation
PO Box 2476
Columbus, OH 43266-0076
Tel: 614-846-6712 **Fax**: 614-466-6401

Oklahoma
Department of Revenue
Income Tax Division
Connors Building, 5th Floor
PO Box 53403
Oklahoma City, OK 73152-3160
Tel: 405-521-3403 **Fax**: 405-521-2035

Oregon
Department of Revenue
955 Center Street N.E.
Revenue Building, #135
Salem, OR 97310
Tel: 503-945-8210 **Fax**: Not Released

Pennsylvania
Pennsylvania Department of Revenue
Bureau of Administrative Services
Central Records Division
12th Floor, Strawberry Square
Harrisburg, PA 17128-1200
Tel: 717-787-3683 **Fax**: Not Released

Rhode Island
Department of Administration
Division of Taxation
One Capitol Hill
Providence, RI 02908
Tel: 401-277-2905 **Fax**: 401-277-6006

South Carolina
State of South Carolina
Department of Revenue and Taxation
301 Gervais Street
Columbia, SC 29201
Tel: 803-737-4766 **Fax**: 803-737-4898

Tennessee
Department of Revenue
Andrew Jackson State Office Building
500 Deaderick Street
Nashville, TN 37242
Tel: 615-741-3580 **Fax**: 615-532-6396

Texas
No state income tax.

Utah
Tax Commission
Hever M. Wells Building
210 N. 1950 West
Salt Lake City, UT 84134
Tel: 801-297-2200 **Fax**: Not Released

Vermont
State of Vermont
Department of Taxes
109 State Street
Montpelier, VT 05609-1401
Tel: 802-828-2865 **Fax**: Not Released

Virginia
Tax Commission
Department of Taxation
PO Box 1115
Richmond, VA 23218-1115
Tel: 804-367-8031 **Fax**: 804-367-0985

Washington
No state income tax.

West Virginia
Department of Tax and Revenue
Tax Division
PO Box 3784
Charleston, WV 25337-3784
Tel: 304-558-3333 Fax: 304-558-3269

Wisconsin
State of Wisconsin
Department of Revenue
Income, Sale and Excise Tax Division
Revenue Audit Bureau
PO Box 8903
Madison, WI 53708-8903
Tel: 608-266-2890 **Fax**: Not Released

Wyoming
No state income tax.

United States - Federal Agencies

In addition to the fifty states, the District of Columbia and Puerto Rico, numerous federal agencies also hold unclaimed money and property.

Contacting federal agencies is no different than contacting state agencies. However, where a state agency has gathered unclaimed property information from many sources within the state, i.e. banks, savings and loans, insurance companies, utility companies, etc., each federal agency is specific with regard to the origin of its unclaimed money or property.

The following pages provide contact information for federal agencies of the United States inclusive of mailing and Internet address, telephone and facsimile numbers for each agency. Later in this guide you will find a sample letter which you may wish to use as a template for your inquiry requests to these agencies.

Bureau of the Public Debt

The Bureau of Public Debt sells Treasury bills, notes, and bonds, as well as U.S. Savings Bonds; pays interest to investors; and, when the time comes to pay back the loans, redeems investors' securities.

Bureau of the Public Debt
Capital Area Servicing Center
1300 C Street, S.W.
Washington, DC 20239-0001

Telephone: 202-874-4000
Facsimile: Not released

Internet address
WWW: http://www.unclaimed-property.com

Agency: http://www.publicdebt.treas.gov
E-mail: Various - see web site

Internal Revenue Service

The Internal Revenue Service currently holds millions of dollars in undeliverable tax refunds.

Internal Revenue Service offices by areas served:

Atlanta, GA 39901
Telephone: 404-455-2360
Serves Florida, Georgia, South Carolina

Holtsville, NY 00501
Telephone: 516-447-4955
Serves New Jersey, New York City and counties of Nassau, Rockland, Suffolk and Westchester

Andover, MA 05501
Telephone: 508-474-9717
Serves New York (all other counties), Connecticut, Maine, Massachusetts, New Hampshire, Rhode Island, Vermont

Kansas City, MO 64999
Telephone: 816-926-5999
Serves Illinois, Iowa, Minnesota, Missouri, Wisconsin

Philadelphia, PA 19255
Telephone: 215-516-6999
Serves Delaware, District of Columbia, Maryland, Pennsylvania, Virginia

Cincinnati, OH 45999
Telephone: 606-292-5467
Serves Indiana, Kentucky, Michigan, Ohio, West Virginia

Austin, TX 73301
Telephone: 512-462-7843
Serves Kansas, New Mexico, Oklahoma, Texas

Ogden, UT 84201
Telephone: 801-620-7645
Serves Alaska, Arizona, California (counties of Alpine, Amador, Butte, Calaveras Colusa, Contra, Costa, Del Norte, El Dorado, Glenn, Humboldt, Lake, Lassen, Marin, Mendocino, Modoc, Napa, Nevada, Placer, Plumas, Sacramento, San Joaquin, Shasta, Sierra, Siskiyou, Solano, Sonoma, Sutter, Tehama, Trinity, Yolo and Yubal), Colorado, Idaho, Montana, Nebraska, Nevada, North Dakota, Oregon, South Dakota, Utah, Washington, Wyoming

Fresno, CA 93888
Telephone: 209-452-4010
Serves California (all other counties), Hawaii

Memphis, TN 37501
Telephone: 901-365-5970
Serves Alabama, Arkansas, Louisiana, Mississippi, North Carolina, Tennessee

General Inquiries

Telephone: 800-829-1040
Facsimile: Not released

Internet address

WWW: http://www.unclaimed-property.com

Agency: http://www.irs.ustreas.gov
E-mail: Various - see web site

Social Security Administration

The Social Security Administration recently outlined over **200 million** wage reports which it has been unable to match to the appropriate social security benefactors - over **$234 billion**.

Take advantage of their PEBES program, **Personal Earnings and Benefit Estimate Statement**, which shows your Social Security earnings history and how much Social Security taxes you have paid into the program. It also estimates your future benefits and tells you how to qualify for those benefits. PEBES does NOT include current salary or detailed earnings information, such as employer's names or addresses. PEBES is a free service.

Social Security Administration
Department of Health and Human Services
6401 Security Boulevard
Baltimore, MD 21235

Telephone: 410-965-7700
Facsimile: Not released

Internet address
WWW: http://www.unclaimed-property.com

Agency: http://www.ssa.gov
E-mail: Various - see web site

U.S. Department of Labor

This Pension Benefit Guaranty Corporation holds the names of people who have worked long enough to earn a pension benefit, but could no longer be located by their companies. Although the Pension Benefit Guaranty Corporation has been successful in reuniting many people with their missing pensions, there are still numerous individuals who have not been located.

U.S. Department of Labor
Pension Benefit Guaranty Corporation
1200 K Street, N.W.
Washington, DC 2005-4026

Telephone: 202-326-4040
800-400-7242
Facsimile: Not released

Internet address
WWW: http://www.unclaimed-property.com

Agency: http://www.pbgc.gov
E-mail: missing@pbgc.gov

U.S. Department of Public Housing and Urban Development

When FHA mortgage insurance is terminated prior to the term of the insured loan, a portion of the insurance collected MAY be refundable to the homeowner if the mortgage was held for less than 84 months. HUD uses various methods to locate homeowners including: mailing refund notifications, sending occupant letters to the property address, inquiring to credit bureaus, and postal change of address files.

U.S. Department of Public Housing & Urban Development
HUD Mortgage Insurance
PO Box 9500
Springfield, VA 22151

Telephone: 703-487-4070
Facsimile: Not released

Internet address
WWW: http://www.unclaimed-property.com

Agency: http://www.hud.gov
E-mail: Various - see web site

United States - Life Insurance Companies

Across the United States, life insurance policy owners and beneficiaries sometimes become separated from their insurance agent, agency or company. This happens most often when the insurance company is not provided with necessary name and address changes.

Insurance companies go to great lengths to locate owners of unclaimed monies. However, if after a thorough search, the insurance company is unable to locate a policy beneficiary, money that is rightfully owed to that person reverts to the state for safe keeping within three to five years (depending upon the policy type and state).

The American Council of Life Insurance has released the following list representing thc top fifty life insurance companies. Contact information is provided should you believe you may be entitled to specific life insurance benefits directly or as a beneficiary which have not reverted to a state agency as of yet.

American Council of Life Insurance

American Council of Life Insurance
1001 Pennsylvania Avenue, NW
Washington, DC 20004-2599

Telephone: (202)624-2000
Facsimile: (202)624-2319

Internet address

WWW: http://www.acli.com
E-mail: Pending

Individual Life Insurance Companies

AIG Life Insurance Company
One Alico Plaza
Wilmington, DE 19801
Telephone: (302) 594-2000

Allianz Life Insurance Company of North America
1750 Hennepin Avenue
Minneapolis, MN 55403-2195
Telephone: (612) 347-6500

Allstate Life Insurance Company
3100 Sanders Road
Northbrook, IL 60062
Telephone: (847) 402-5000

American General Life & Accident Insurance Company
American General Center
Nashville, TN 37250
Telephone: (615) 749-1000

American Life Insurance Company
PO Box 2226
Wilmington, DE 19899
Telephone: (302) 594-2000

American United Life Insurance Company
PO Box 368
Indianapolis, IN 46206-0368
Telephone: (317) 263-1877

Business Men's Assurance Company of America
PO Box 419458
Kansas City, MO 64141
Telephone: (816) 753-8000

Chubb Life Insurance Company of America
One Granite Place
Concord, NH 03301-3258
Telephone: (603) 226-5000

Connecticut General Life Insurance Company
900 Cottage Grove Road
Bloomfield, CT 06002
Telephone: (860) 726-6000

Continental Assurance Company
CNA Plaza, 22 South
Chicago, IL 60685
Telephone: (312) 822-5000

Equitable Life Assurance Society of the United States
787 Seventh Avenue, 49th Floor
New York, NY 10019
Telephone: (212) 554-1234

Equitable Variable Life Insurance Company
787 Seventh Avenue, 49th Floor
New York, NY 10019
Telephone: (212) 641-8342

Farmers New World Insurance Company
3003 77th Avenue SE
Mercer Island, WA 98040
Telephone: (206) 232-8400

Federal Kemper Life Assurance Company
One Kemper Drive, T-1
Long Grove, IL 60049
Telephone: (847) 550-5500

First Colony Life Insurance Company
PO Box 1280
Lynchburg, VA 24505
Telephone: (804) 845-0911

General American Life Insurance Company
PO Box 396
St. Louis, MO 63166
Telephone: (314) 843-8700

Guardian Life Insurance Company of America
201 Park Avenue South
New York, NY 10003
Telephone: (212) 598-8000

Hartford Life Insurance Company
PO Box 2999
Hartford, CT 06104-2999
Telephone: (860) 843-8291

IDS Life Insurance Company
IDS Tower 10
Minneapolis, MN 55440-0010
Telephone: (612) 671-3131

Jackson National Life Insurance Company
5901 Executive Drive
Lansing, MI 48911
Telephone: (517) 394-3400

Jefferson-Pilot Life Insurance Company
PO Box 21008
Greensboro, NC 24720
Telephone: (910) 691-3000

John Hancock Mutual Life Insurance Company
PO Box 111
Boston, MA 02117
Telephone: (617) 572-6000

John Hancock Variable Life Insurance Company
PO Box 717
Boston, MA 02117
Telephone: (617) 572-6000

Lincoln National Life Insurance Company
1300 South Clinton Street
Fort Wayne, IN 46801
Telephone: (219) 455-2000

Massachusetts Mutual Life Insurance Company
1295 State Street
Springfield, MA 01111
Telephone: (413) 788-8411

MBL Life Assurance Corporation
520 Broad Street
Newark, NJ 07102-3111
Telephone: (201) 481-8000

Metropolitan Insurance & Annuity Company
One Madison Avenue, Area 9H
New York, NY 10010
Telephone: (212) 578-2211

Metropolitan Life Insurance Company
One Madison Avenue, Area 9H
New York, NY 10010-3690
Telephone: (212) 578-2211

Midland National Life Insurance Company
One Midland Plaza
Sioux Falla, SD 57193-0001
Telephone: (605) 335-5700

Minnesota Mutual Life Insurance Company
Minnesota Mutual Center, 400 Robert Street North
St. Paul, MN 55101
Telephone: (612) 298-3500

Mutual Life Insurance Company of New York
1740 Broadway at 55th Street
New York, NY 10019
Telephone: (212) 708-2000

New York Life Insurance & Annuity Corporation
51 Madison Avenue
New York, NY 10010
Telephone: (212) 576-7000

New York Life Insurance Company
51 Madison Avenue
New York, NY 10010
Telephone: (212) 576-7000

North American Company for Life & Health Insuranc
PO Box 466
Chicago, IL 60690-0466
Telephone: (312) 648-7600

Northwestern Mutual Life Insurance Company
720 East Wisconsin Avenue
Milwaukee, WI 53202
Telephone: (414) 271-1444

Old Line Life Insurance Company of America
PO Box 401
Milwaukee, WI 53201-0401
Telephone: (414) 271-2820

Pacific Mutual Life Insurance Company
700 Newport Center Drive
Newport Beach, CA 92660
Telephone: (714) 640-3011

Phoenix Home Life Mutual Insurance Company
100 Bright Meadow Boulevard
Einfield, CT 06083-1900
Telephone: (518) 479-8000

Primerica Life Insurance Company
3120 Breckinridge Boulevard
Duluth, GA 30199-0001
Telephone: (404) 381-1000

Principal Mutual Life Insurance Company
711 High Street
Des Moines, IA 50392-0120
Telephone: (515) 247-5111

Protective Life Insurance Company
PO Box 2606
Birmingham, AL 35202
Telephone: (205) 879-9230

Prudential Insurance Company of America
Prudential Plaza
Newark, NJ 07102-2992
Telephone: (201) 802-6000

Security-Connecticut Life Insurance Company
20 Security Drive
Avon, CT 06001
Telephone: (860) 677-8621

Security Life of Denver Insurance Company
PO Box 105006
Atlanta, GA 30348-5006
Telephone: (303) 860-1290

State Farm Life Insurance Company
One State Farm Plaza
Bloomington, IL 61710
Telephone: (309)766-2311

Transamerica Occidental Life Insurance Company
1150 South Olive Street
Los Angeles, CA 90015
Telephone: (213) 742-2111

Travelers Insurance Company
One Tower Square
Hartford, CT 06183
Telephone: (203) 277-0111

USAA Life Insurance Company
USAA Building
San Antonio, TX 78288
Telephone: (210) 498-8000

Valley Forge Life Insurance Company
CNA Plaza, 22 South
Chicago, IL 60685
Telephone: (312) 822-5000

Western & Southern Life Insurance Company
400 Broadway
Cincinnati, OH 45202
Telephone: (513) 629-1800

(This page intentionally blank)

United States - Railroad Retirement Board

Prospective retirees, spouses and beneficiaries should be aware of what steps to take and what documents are required by the Railroad Retirement Board when inquiring about retirement or life insurance benefits which may be owed them. Contact your regional Railroad Retirement Board office.

Alabama

U.S. Railroad Retirement Board
Medical Forum Building
950 22nd Street North, Room 426
Birmingham, AL 35203-1126
Tel: 205-731-0019 **Fax:** 205-731-0026

Arizona

U.S. Railroad Retirement Board
USPO/Federal Building, Room 221
PO Box 13206 522 N. Central
Phoenix, AZ 85002-3206
Tel: 602-379-4841 **Fax:** 602-379-3798

Arkansas

U.S. Railroad Retirement Board
1200 Cherry Brook Drive, Suite 500
Little Rock, AR 72211-4113
Tel: 501-324-5241 **Fax:** 501-324-7159

California

U.S. Railroad Retirement Board
801 I Street, Room 205
Sacramento, CA 95814-2510
Tel: 916-498-6654 **Fax:** 916-498-6659

California (continued)

U.S. Railroad Retirement Board
Oakland Federal Building
1301 Clay Street Suite 392 N
Oakland, CA 94612-5220
Tel: 510-637-2973 **Fax:** 510-637-2978

U.S. Railroad Retirement Board
Building B, Suite 360
1515 West Cameron Avenue
West Covina, CA 91790-2726
Tel: 626-814-8844 **Fax:** 626-814-1219

Colorado

U.S. Railroad Retirement Board
721 19th Street, Room 177
PO Box 8869
Denver, CO 80201-8869
Tel: 303-844-4311 **Fax:** 303-391-5869

Florida

U.S. Railroad Retirement Board
Bennett Federal Building
400 W. Bay Street, Room 315
PO Box 35026
Jacksonville, FL 32202-4412
Tel: 904-232-2546 **Fax:** 904-232-2874

Florida (continued)

U.S. Railroad Retirement Board
Federal Annex Building, Room 100
501 Polk Street
Tampa, FL 33602-3953
Tel: 813-228-2695 **Fax:** 813-228-2939

Georgia

U.S. Railroad Retirement Board
Peachtree Summit Building, Room 1702
401 W Peachtree Street
Atlanta, GA 30365-2550
Tel: 404-331-2841 **Fax:** 404-331-7234

Illinois

U.S. Railroad Retirement Board
844 N. Rush Street
Ninth Floor
Chicago, IL 60611-2092
Tel: 312-751-4500 **Fax:** 312-751-7136

U.S. Railroad Retirement Board
Millikin Court
132 S. Water Street, Suite 517
Decatur, IL 62523-1397
Tel: 217-423-9747 **Fax:** 217-423-7872

Illinois (continued)

U.S. Railroad Retirement Board
101 N. Joliet Street, Room 120
PO Box 457
Joliet, IL 60434-0457
Tel: 815-740-2101 **Fax:** 815-740-2139

Indiana

U.S. Railroad Retirement Board
The Meridian Centre
50 S. Meridian, Suite 303
Indianapolis, IN 46204-3530
Tel: 317-226-6111 **Fax:** 317-226-5374

Iowa

U.S. Railroad Retirement Board
Federal Building
210 Walnut Street, Room 921
Des Moines, IA 50309-2182
Tel: 515-284-4344 **Fax:** 515-284-4616

Kansas

U.S. Railroad Retirement Board
UNISYS Building, Suite 390
1861 N. Rock Road
Wichita, KS 67206-1264
Tel: 316-687-5973 **Fax:** 316-687-3572

Kentucky

U.S. Railroad Retirement Board
Theatre Building
629 S. 4th Avenue, Suite 301
PO Box 3705
Louisville, KY 40201-3705
Tel: 502-582-5208 **Fax:** 502-582-5518

Louisiana

U.S. Railroad Retirement Board
501 Magazine Street, Room 1046
New Orleans, LA 70130-3394
Tel: 504-589-2597 **Fax:** 504-589-4899

Maryland

U.S. Railroad Retirement Board
300 West Pratt Street, Room 260
Baltimore, MD 21201-2803
Tel: 410-962-2550 **Fax:** 410-962-9835

Massachusetts

U.S. Railroad Retirement Board
121 High Street, Room 301
PO Box 2448
Boston, MA 02208-2448
Tel: 617-424-5790 **Fax:** 617-424-5795

Michigan

U.S. Railroad Retirement Board
McNamara Federal Building
477 W. Michigan Avenue, Suite 1990
Detroit, MI 48226-2596
Tel: 313-226-6221 **Fax:** 313-226-4233

Minnesota

U.S. Railroad Retirement Board
Federal Building Room 125
515 W. First Street
Duluth, MN 55802-1392
Tel: 218-720-5301 **Fax:** 218-720-5329

U.S. Railroad Retirement Board
First Trust Center, Suite 195, 1st Floor
180 E. 5th Street
St. Paul, MN 55101-1631
Tel: 612-290-3491 **Fax:** 612-290-3076

Missouri

U.S. Railroad Retirement Board
Federal Building, Room 258
601 E. 12th Street
Kansas City, MO 64106-2882
Tel: 816-426-5884 **Fax:** 816-426-5334

Missouri (continued)

U.S. Railroad Retirement Board
Young Federal Building
1222 Spruce Street, Room 1213
St. Louis, MO 63103-2818
Tel: 314-539-6220 **Fax:** 314-539-6229

Montana

U.S. Railroad Retirement Board
Judge Jameson Federal Building
2900 Fourth Avenue North, Room 101
Billings, MT 59101-1266
Tel: 406-247-7375 **Fax:** 406-247-7379

Nebraska

U.S. Railroad Retirement Board
Federal Office Building, Room 1011
106 S. 15th, PO Box 1415
Omaha, NE 68101-1415
Tel: 402-221-4641 **Fax:** 402-221-4669

New Jersey

U.S. Railroad Retirement Board
Rodino Federal Building
970 Broad Street, Room 1435B
Newark, NJ 07102-2518
Tel: 201-645-3990 **Fax:** 201-645-3373

New Mexico

U.S. Railroad Retirement Board
300 San Mateo Northeast, Room 401
Albuquerque, NM 87108-1520
Tel: 505-262-6405 **Fax:** 505-262-6407

New York

U.S. Railroad Retirement Board
Leo W. O'Brien Federal Building, Room 264
Clinton Avenue & Pearl Street, PO Box 529
Albany, NY 12201-0529
Tel: 518-431-4004 **Fax:** 518-431-4000

U.S. Railroad Retirement Board
Dulski Federal Building
111 W. Huron, Room 1106
Buffalo, NY 14202-2394
Tel: 716-551-4141 **Fax:** 716-551-3802

U.S. Railroad Retirement Board
1400 Old Country Road, Suite 204
Westbury, NY 11590-5119
Tel: 516-334-5940 **Fax:** 406-247-7379

U.S. Railroad Retirement Board
Federal Building
26 Federal Plaza Room 3404
New York, NY 10278-0105
Tel: 212-264-9820 **Fax:** 212-264-1687

North Carolina

U.S. Railroad Retirement Board
Mart Office Building
800 Briar Creek Road, Room AA-405
Charlotte, NC 28205-6903
Tel: 704-344-6118 **Fax:** 704-344-6429

North Dakota

U.S. Railroad Retirement Board
USPO Building, Room 343
657 Second Avenue North, PO Box 383
Fargo, ND 58107-0383
Tel: 701-239-5117 **Fax:** 701-239-5261

Ohio

U.S. Railroad Retirement Board
CBLD Center Room 201
36 East 7th Street
Cincinnati, OH 45202-4439
Tel: 513-684-3188 **Fax:** 513-684-3182

U.S. Railroad Retirement Board
Celebrezze Federal Building
1240 E. 9th Street, Room 907
Cleveland, OH 44199-2093
Tel: 216-522-4053 **Fax:** 216-522-2320

Oregon

U.S. Railroad Retirement Board
Green-Wyatt Federal Building, Room 377
1220 SW 3rd Avenue
Portland, OR 97204-2807
Tel: 503-326-2143 **Fax:** 503-326-2157

Pennsylvania

U.S. Railroad Retirement Board
615 Howard Avenue, Room 209
PO Box 990
Altoona, PA 16603-0990
Tel: 814-946-3601 **Fax:** 814-946-3620

U.S. Railroad Retirement Board
228 Walnut Street Room 504
Box 576
Harrisburg, PA 17108-1697
Tel: 717-221-4490 **Fax:** 717-221-3364

U.S. Railroad Retirement Board
1421 Cherry Street, Suite 660
Philadelphia, PA 19102-1493
Tel: 215-656-6993 **Fax:** 215-656-6996

U.S. Railroad Retirement Board
Kossman Building, Room 1130
100 Forbes Avenue
Pittsburgh, PA 15222-1311
Tel: 412-644-2696 **Fax:** 412-391-7689

Pennsylvania (continued)

U.S. Railroad Retirement Board
Siniawa Plaza II, Route 6
717 Scranton/Carbondale Highway
Scranton, PA 18508-1121
Tel: 717-346-5774   **Fax:** 717-346-6042

Tennessee

U.S. Railroad Retirement Board
233 Cumberland Bend Drive, Suite 206
Nashville, TN 37228-1813
Tel: 615-736-5131   **Fax:** 615-736-7071

Texas

U.S. Railroad Retirement Board
Leland Federal Building Suite 845
1919 Smith
Houston, TX 77002-8051
Tel: 713-209-3045   **Fax:** 713-209-3044

U.S. Railroad Retirement Board
819 Taylor Street, Room 10G02
PO Box 17420
Ft. Worth, TX 76102-0420
Tel: 817-978-2638   **Fax:** 817-978-2740

Utah

U.S. Railroad Retirement Board
Bennett Federal Building Room 1205
125 S. State
Salt Lake City, UT 84138-1102
Tel: 801-524-5725 **Fax:** 801-524-4313

Virginia

U.S. Railroad Retirement Board
Suite 232, 2nd Floor
704 E. Franklin Street
Richmond, VA 23219-2313
Tel: 804-771-2997 **Fax:** 804-771-8481

U.S. Railroad Retirement Board
First Campbell Square, Suite 460
210 First Street Southwest, PO Box 270
Roanoke, VA 24002-0270
Tel: 540-857-2335 **Fax:** 540-857-2769

Washington

U.S. Railroad Retirement Board
U.S. Courthouse, Room 492
W. 920 Riverside Avenue
Spokane, WA 99201-1081
Tel: 509-353-2795 **Fax:** 509-353-2741

Washington (continued)

U.S. Railroad Retirement Board
Pacific First Plaza, Suite 201
155 108th Avenue Northeast
Bellevue, WA 98004-5901
Tel: 206-553-5483 **Fax:** 206-553-0179

West Virginia

U.S. Railroad Retirement Board
New Federal Building, Room 112
640 4th Avenue, PO Box 2153
Huntington, WV 25721-2153
Tel: 304-529-5561 **Fax:** 304-529-5546

Wisconsin

U.S. Railroad Retirement Board
Reuss Federal Plaza, Suite 1300
310 W. Wisconsin Avenue
Milwaukee, WI 53203-2211
Tel: 414-297-3961 **Fax:** 414-297-3833

International Unclaimed Property Resources

Additional unclaimed money and property resources from throughout the world are being researched, identified and added to **The Unclaimed Property Resource Guide©** and **The National Unclaimed Property Database©** on our Internet site at **http://www.unclaimed-property.com**.

While state and federal agencies of the United States have been our primary focus to date; we are currently identifying resources in Canada, Australia, South America and European countries.

Bank of Canada

The Bank of Canada maintains a centralized file of abandoned or unclaimed bank accounts from banks throughout the Provinces of Canada.

Bank of Canada
Comptroller's Department
234 Wellington Street
Ottawa, ON K1A 0G9

Telephone: 204-945-0513
Facsimile: Not released

Internet address
WWW: http://www.unclaimed-property.com

Agency: Pending
E-mail: Pending

Swiss Bankers Association

On June 25, 1997, the Swiss Federal Banking Commission, Switzerland's bank supervisory authority, ordered that accounts dormant since the end of World War II be made public to assist claimants, including Holocaust victims and their heirs, locate assets that belong to them. The accounts being published are those that were opened by non-Swiss - people whose nationality or domicile was not Swiss - and have been dormant since the end of World War II (May 9, 1945). Dormant accounts opened by Swiss persons prior to the end of World War II are also now available.

Swiss Bankers Association
c/o Ernst & Young, LLP
"Dormant Accounts"
PO Box 1880 Radio City Station
New York, NY 10101-1880

Telephone: 212-344-0610
800-662-7708
Facsimile: Not released

Internet address
WWW: http://www.unclaimed-property.com

Agency: http://www.dormantaccounts.ch
E-mail: Not released

(This page intentionally blank)

Section III:

Start your search TODAY!

(This page intentionally blank)

Sample Agency Contact Letter

The following letter may be used as an outline for your inquiries:

John Fitzgerald Doe
12345 SW 67 Street
Anytown, USA 12345

July 23, 1996

AGENCY NAME
AGENCY ADDRESS
AGENCY CITY, AGENCY STATE AGENCY ZIP CODE

Dear **AGENCY NAME**:

Please search your records of unclaimed and abandoned property regarding any money or property you may be holding in my name:

Name:	John Fitzgerald Doe
Current Address:	12345 SW 67 Street Anytown, USA 12345
Previous Address:	8910 Willow Court Anycity, USA 67890
SSN:	012-34-5678

Please feel free to contact me at (123) 456-7890 should you need any further information. Thank you in advance for your assistance.

(This page intentionally blank)

Inquiry Service Forms

Should you not want to spend the time writing or calling over fifty agencies - **we will do it for you**.

Knowledge In Motion® will send out correspondence on your behalf to all fifty U.S. state agencies, the District of Columbia and Puerto Rico. The correspondence will request that they search their records for money and property which may belong to you individually, as a co-owner or as an inheritance. The agencies will then respond or contact you directly beginning in about two weeks.

To utilize this service, complete the enclosed **Inquiry Service Form** (or a photocopy), enclose payment information and forward to:

Knowledge In Motion®, Inc.
1825 Ponce de Leon Blvd., Suite 239
Coral Gables, Florida 33134-4418

One individual or business per inquiry form please. All information submitted is deemed confidential and will be used only for the purposes explained herein.

(This page intentionally blank)

☐ **YES!** Please contact the fifty U.S. state agencies, the District of Columbia and Puerto Rico on my behalf. Request that they search their records for my name and forward all responses to me directly.

Cost: $19.95 (includes correspondence and postage)
Payment method:

☐ Check payable to Knowledge In Motion®, Inc.

☐ American Express ☐ Discover ☐ MasterCard ☐ Visa

Account: ______________________________ Exp. ______

Name on account: ______________________________

Signature: ______________________________

Search information: (please print or type)

NAME: ______________________________
(First) (Middle) (Last)

MAIDEN NAME (if applicable): ______________________________

CURRENT ADDRESS: ______________________________
(Street)

____
(City) (State) (Zip)

PREVIOUS ADDRESS: ______________________________

DAYTIME PHONE: ____________ **DATE OF BIRTH**: ____/____/____

SOCIAL SECURITY NUMBER: ______-______-______

For **additional** orders, photocopy this form and submit separate payment for each individual or business. All information submitted is deemed confidential and will be used only for the purposes explained herein. Forward completed form and payment to: **Knowledge In Motion®, Inc., 1825 Ponce de Leon Blvd., Suite 239, Coral Gables, Florida 33134-4418.**

(This page intentionally blank)

☐ **YES!** Please contact the fifty U.S. state agencies, the District of Columbia and Puerto Rico on my behalf. Request that they search their records for my name and forward all responses to me directly.

Cost: $19.95 (includes correspondence and postage)
Payment method:

☐ Check payable to Knowledge In Motion®, Inc.

☐ American Express ☐ Discover ☐ MasterCard ☐ Visa

Account: ______________________________ Exp. ______

Name on account: ______________________________

Signature: ______________________________

Search information: (please print or type)

NAME: ______________________________
(First) (Middle) (Last)

MAIDEN NAME (if applicable): ______________________________

CURRENT ADDRESS: ______________________________
(Street)
____
(City) (State) (Zip)

PREVIOUS ADDRESS: ______________________________

DAYTIME PHONE: ______________ **DATE OF BIRTH**: ____/____/____

SOCIAL SECURITY NUMBER: ________-______-________

For **additional** orders, photocopy this form and submit separate payment for each individual or business. All information submitted is deemed confidential and will be used only for the purposes explained herein. Forward completed form and payment to: **Knowledge In Motion®, Inc., 1825 Ponce de Leon Blvd., Suite 239, Coral Gables, Florida 33134-4418.**

(This page intentionally blank)

Tips for Safekeeping your Financial Assets

- Keep accurate financial records. Record all bank accounts, stock certificates, insurance policies, utility and rent deposits, and your safe deposit box number.

- Have interest posted for savings accounts at least every two to three years.

- Make sure to cash all checks for dividends, insurance benefits and wages.

- Notify a family member or trusted advisor of the location of your records.

- Prepare a checklist of these items in order to notify all concerned parties if you change your address.

(This page intentionally blank)